NATURE'S GIANTS

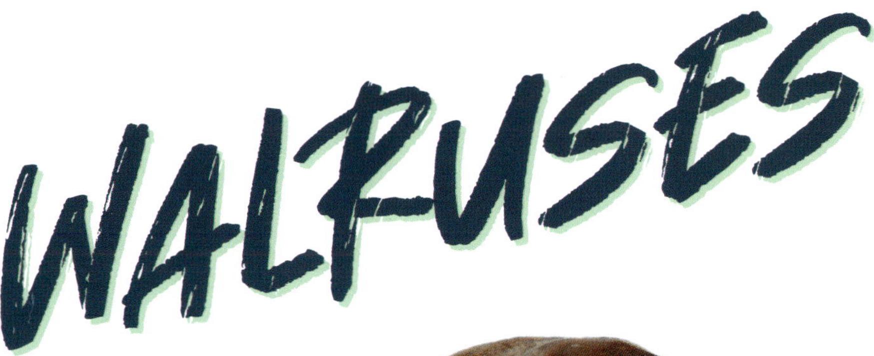

WALRUSES

BY MARISSA KIRKMAN

WWW.APEXEDITIONS.COM

Apex is distributed by North Star Editions:
sales@northstareditions.com | 888-417-0195

Produced for Apex by Red Line Editorial.

Photographs ©: iStockphoto, cover, 22–23; Shutterstock Images, 1, 4–5, 6, 8–9, 12, 13, 14–15, 16–17, 18, 19, 24, 25, 26–27, 29; Johner Images/Alamy, 7; Kevin Elsby/Alamy, 10–11; Axel Heimken/picture-alliance/dpa/AP Images, 20–21

Library of Congress Control Number: 2023924596

ISBN
978-1-63738-941-6 (hardcover)
978-1-63738-981-2 (paperback)
979-8-89250-075-3 (ebook pdf)
979-8-89250-039-5 (hosted ebook)

Printed in the United States of America
Mankato, MN
082024

NOTE TO PARENTS AND EDUCATORS

Apex books are designed to build literacy skills in striving readers. Exciting, high-interest content attracts and holds readers' attention. The text is carefully leveled to allow students to achieve success quickly. Additional features, such as bolded glossary words for difficult terms, help build comprehension.

TABLE OF CONTENTS

CHAPTER 1

DIVING FOR CLAMS

A walrus swims down to the seafloor. She searches for food with her **snout**. Her **whiskers** feel some clams.

Walruses have hundreds of whiskers on their faces.

The walrus wraps her lips around a clam's shell. She sucks out the clam. Then she eats several more.

Clams often live in shallow, sandy water.

Walruses suck in and push out water with their mouths. This moves sand and uncovers food.

FINDING FOOD

To find food, walruses swim along the seafloor. They use their snouts or flippers to move sand. Animals hiding under the sand come out. Walruses eat them.

The walrus swims up to the surface for air. She finds a patch of sea ice. She uses her **tusks** to pull her body up onto the ice. The walrus lies there until she gets hungry again.

Walruses use sea ice to rest while feeding and traveling.

CHAPTER 2

BIG BODIES

Walruses are massive **mammals**. They can weigh up to 3,750 pounds (1,700 kg). Their bodies can grow up to 12 feet (4 m) long.

Male walruses can be twice as big as females.

Male walruses may fight over females or good resting spots.

Walruses have long tusks. Walruses use their tusks to fight. Tusks also help them climb onto ice or poke holes in ice to breathe.

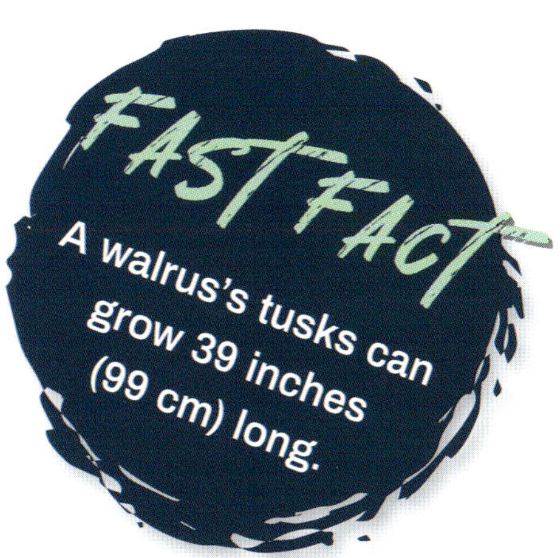

Female walruses tend to have shorter tusks than males.

Walruses' rough skin helps them move on ice without slipping.

THICK SKIN

Walruses have rough, thick skin. A layer of fat called blubber is underneath. This fat can be up to 4 inches (10 cm) thick. It keeps walruses warm in icy water.

Walruses have strong flippers. The back flippers help walruses swim quickly. The front flippers help them change directions. Walruses can also use their flippers to walk on land.

CHAPTER 3

LIFE IN THE WATER

Walruses live in shallow **Arctic** seas. They often stay near coasts and sea ice. But they spend most of their lives in the water.

Walruses live in very cold areas. Lying close together helps them stay warm.

Atlantic walruses are slightly smaller than Pacific walruses.

There are two main types of walruses. Pacific walruses **migrate** north in the summer and south in the winter. Atlantic walruses stay near rocky beaches all year.

MELTING ICE

Climate change is causing sea ice to melt. Walruses must swim farther to find places to rest. Thousands may crowd onto the same shores. They can get hurt or run out of food.

Walruses may crush one another on crowded beaches.

Walruses typically have two meals every day.

Walruses eat up to 110 pounds (50 kg) of food each day. They mainly eat clams, snails, crabs, and shrimp. But they sometimes eat fish, too.

FAST FACT

Walruses can eat between 3,000 and 6,000 clams in one meal.

CHAPTER 4

HUGE HERDS

Walruses live in herds. Some herds have just a few walruses. Other groups include more than 1,000. Males and females live in different herds.

The biggest walrus with the longest tusks is usually the leader of each herd.

Females have one calf every two to three years. They give birth on sea ice. Mothers feed and care for their babies.

Female walruses hold their babies with their flippers.

Walruses are hunted by orcas, polar bears, and people.

STAYING SAFE

Walrus mothers protect their calves. A calf often swims near its mother's chest or back. This helps her keep it safe. Mothers also use their tusks to fight off **predators**.

FAST FACT
Walruses are noisy animals. They grunt, bark, and whistle.

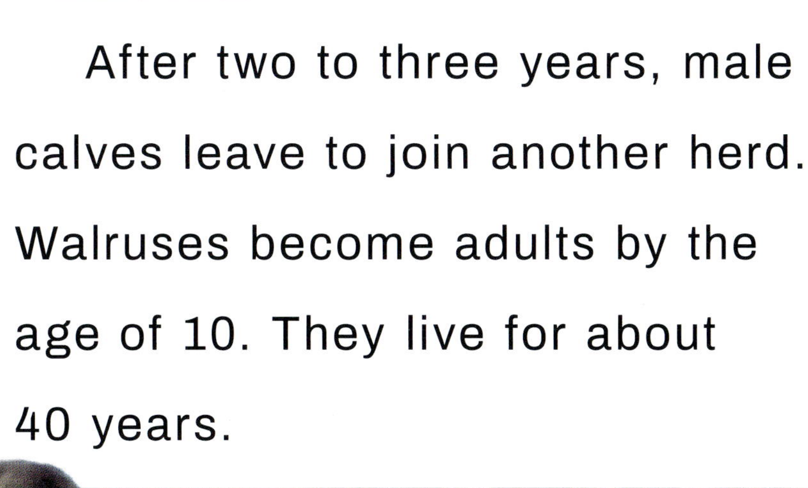

After two to three years, male calves leave to join another herd. Walruses become adults by the age of 10. They live for about 40 years.

A female calf typically stays in the same herd as its mother.

COMPREHENSION QUESTIONS

Write your answers on a separate piece of paper.

1. Write a sentence that explains the main idea of Chapter 2.

2. Would you like to live in the Arctic like walruses do? Why or why not?

3. Which type of walrus migrates north in summer?

   A. Pacific walrus
   B. Atlantic walrus
   C. baby walrus

4. What problem does melting sea ice cause for walruses?

   A. The walruses must stay farther apart.
   B. The walruses have fewer places to rest.
   C. The walruses have too much food to eat.

5. What does **massive** mean in this book?

*Walruses are **massive** mammals. They can weigh up to 3,750 pounds (1,700 kg).*

- **A.** very large
- **B.** small and weak
- **C.** not heavy

6. What does **include** mean in this book?

*Some herds have just a few walruses. Other groups **include** more than 1,000.*

- **A.** scare away
- **B.** swim under
- **C.** are made up of

Answer key on page 32.

GLOSSARY

Arctic

In the very cold area near the North Pole.

climate change

A dangerous long-term change in Earth's temperature and weather patterns.

mammals

Animals that have hair and produce milk for their young.

migrate

To move from one part of the world to another.

predators

Animals that hunt and eat other animals.

snout

The nose and mouth of an animal.

tusks

Long teeth that stick out of an animal's mouth.

whiskers

Thick hairs around an animal's mouth that help the animal feel its surroundings.

BOOKS

Downs, Kieran. *Polar Bear vs. Walrus*. Minneapolis: Bellwether Media, 2022.

Kirkman, Marissa. *Coldest Climates*. Mendota Heights, MN: Apex Editions, 2024.

Murray, Julie. *Walruses*. Minneapolis: Abdo Publishing, 2020.

ONLINE RESOURCES

Visit **www.apexeditions.com** to find links and resources related to this title.

ABOUT THE AUTHOR

Marissa Kirkman is a writer and editor who lives in Illinois. She enjoys reading about animals, science, and history. Her favorite animals to learn about are sea animals.

INDEX

ANSWER KEY:
1. Answers will vary; 2. Answers will vary; 3. A; 4. B; 5. A; 6. C